Shoto Clay - Wares from the Lake River Ceramics Horizon of Southwest Washington State

Part 4 - Pipes

David A. Heath
2011

TABLE OF CONTENTS

Shoto Clay - Wares from the
Lake River Ceramics Horizon
of South Washington State

Part 4 - Pipes

David A. Heath

ABSTRACT

This paper is the fourth of several that have been proposed with an aim of contributing to the body of knowledge related to the subject of ceramic wares, which have been recovered from the Lower Columbia River region in Southwest Washington State and are commonly referred to as Shoto Clay or Lake River Ceramics. Previous research and reporting on this subject has been limited due to a lack of professionally lead excavations and the limited availability of wares from which scientific study might be made.

The author, over a span of several years, has attempted to locate privately held collections that contain these wares with a goal of photographing and obtaining basic data. Through various sources and informants, several local area collections were identified. These collections ranged in size but most were limited to only few examples. When permission could be obtained, photographs, measurements and associated information was collected.

These efforts have resulted in identifying several hundred specimens, many of which had not been previously documented. In some instances, previously unknown ware types were additionally identified. This and future papers will serve as a presentation of the author's findings.

ACKNOWLEDGMENTS

First and foremost, I must give an enormous thanks to the numerous individuals, who allowed access to their privately held collections. Without the forbearance and cooperation of these individuals, this and other prepared papers would not have been possible. They gave freely, allowing access to their homes and contributed hours of their time to answer questions during telephone interviews. Their cooperation and support cannot be underestimated nor overlooked.

Dr. Alison Stenger, the Director of Research for the Institute for Archaeological Studies in Portland, openly shared and discussed her research. Countless numbers of corresponds were exchanged, sharing information and ideas, in a manner that was mutually beneficial and in the sprit of cooperation. It was due in large part to Dr. Stenger's encouragement that this and other prepared papers were ultimately prepared and shared.

Kenneth Matsen, joint author of "Shoto Clay: Figurines and Forms from the Lower Columbia," who gave of his time and provided valuable information about Lake River during the 1950s-1960s. He shared his original research notes and photographs; along with those that had been prepared by Robert Slocum. Mr. Matsen is a kindly gentleman whom I'm proud to call a friend.

INTRODUCTION

This is the fourth in a series of papers that will be prepared in the near future and are designed to contribute materially to the subject of Shoto Clay. Out of respect for the work performed by Robert Slocum and Kenneth Matsen; and due to familiarity by the general public, the term Shoto Clay will be referenced, but know that Lake River Ceramics can be interchangeably used. Photographic evidence and basic recorded information was prepared based on specific ware type classifications that have been identified with the Lake River Ceramics Horizon. These include bowls, figurines, pipes, gaming devices, items of personal adornment and miscellaneous wares.

It is the author's intent to avoid offering any theories about who made these wares or why these wares were made. The information will stand alone and it will be up to others to develop their own ideas about the "Who and Why." The author is not a trained archaeologist or anthropologist. So please forgive any omissions and oversights that will surely be noticed. It is hoped the information provided with these papers will have some informational value and benefit the general public and professional communities. The author is particularly interested in providing material support to any student who might have an interest in pursuing the study of these ceramic wares. The author will be happy to share any images and research information with researchers, provided the author's materials are not used for personal monetary gains and the author is provided with a copy of the finished work.

PIPES

The prehistoric peoples who occupied the Lake River region produced a number of unique smoking devices, collectively referred to as "pipes" in this paper. These pipes have been constructed from a homogenous, non-tempered clay paste that contains naturally occurring admixture consisting of fine-grained sand and flecks of mica. Decorative elements include the use of impressions, punctates, incised lines and appliqué. No examples were identified where applied colorants or shell inlay was evident. A significant number of examples exhibited fire clouding on the exterior of the ware, suggesting direct contact with the flame or fuel source during the firing process. It should be noted that indications of actual use, such as clouding - charring of the rim or interior of the pipe bowl was exceedingly rare.

With the exception of a few unique examples, Shoto Clay pipes have a distinctive tubular form. In all cases, the pipe bowl and stem are integrated into a single continuous ware that forms a distinctive horn shape. The pipe bore appears to have been created using a thin reed like object while the ware was pliable. The tubular pipes typically followed prescribed forms with specific distinguishing traits that allowed for further sub-classification. These sub-classifications include Expanding Stem, Effigy, Long Stem and Short Stem. For the Expanding and Short Stem tubular pipes, it was undetermined if the stem served as a shank intended to be fitted into or over a composite stem. All examples of the Long Stem Tubular Pipe featured secondary modification as evidenced by stem scraping around the entire circumference of the stem. This secondary modification suggests the stem may have served as a tenon and was scraped to fit a mortised stem or mouthpiece. The Effigy tubular pipe is zoomorphic and features applied eyes and punctates that are suggestive of nasal openings.

One unique pipe form noted an anthropomorphic-zoomorphic pipe referred to as a "Figural Effigy pipe." There were only three examples of this pipe form identified, suggesting it is relatively rare and may be the result of individual artistic liberty. The pipe bowl is a well-executed figural form and features a shank with a large, circular mortise opening designed to receive a composite stem. One documented example still had the stem, which was constructed from a large diameter bird bone and decorated with incised rings. Another unique pipe form identified employed a short tapered stem body similar to the previously discussed tubular pipes, but differs in that it features an applied bowl positioned on top and at the end of the stem. This pipe form is conceptually somewhat characteristic of later period elbow pipes.

Pipes - Figural Effigy

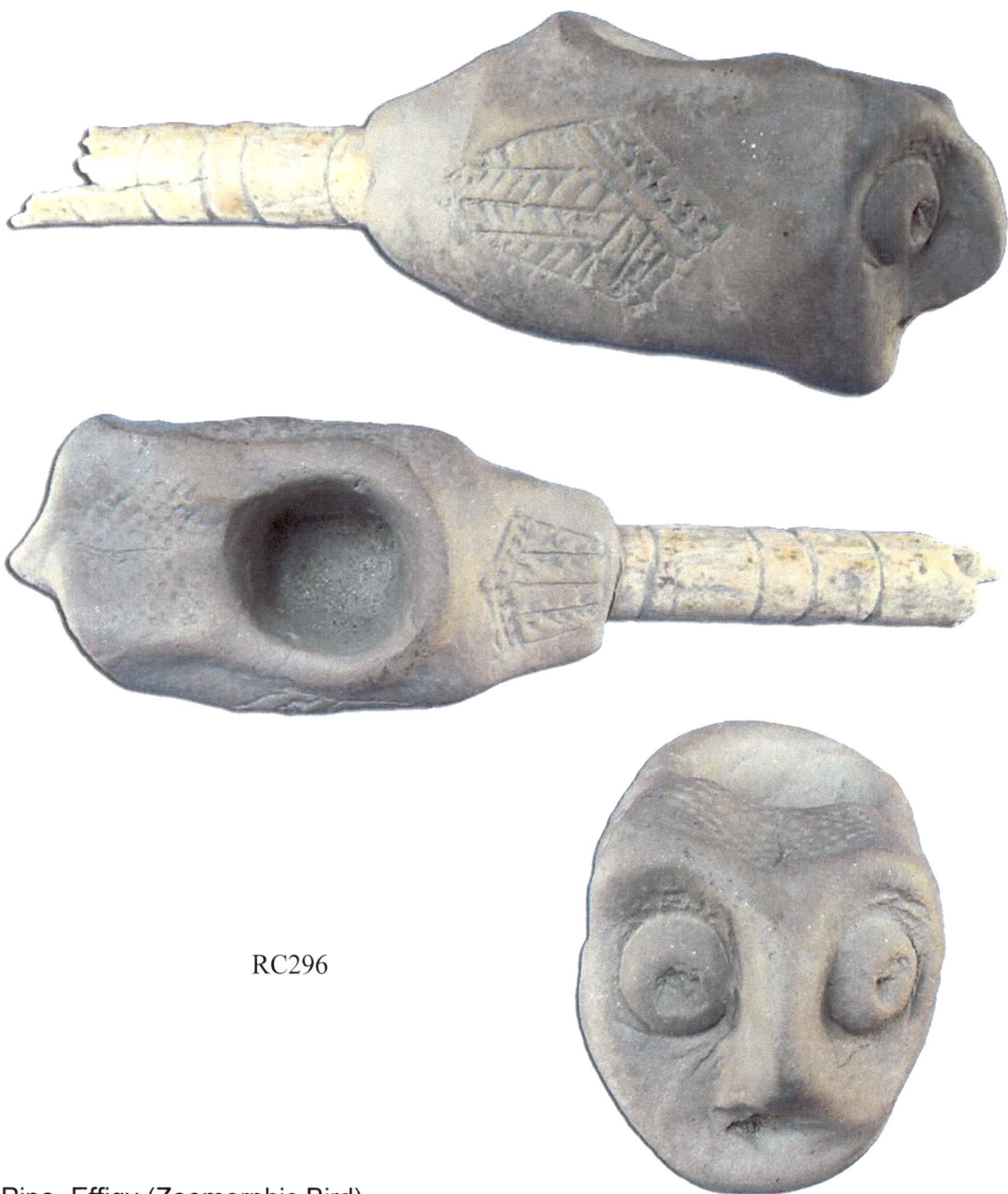

RC296

Pipe, Effigy (Zoomorphic Bird)
Length: 76 mm (with pipe stem 143 mm)
Width: 36 mm
Height: 37 mm
Features incised lines, pinch molding, punctates, mica flakes, an applied slip (or Burnished) finish, fire clouding, the eyes are applied and sculpted. The pipe stem is an incised bird bone and shows remains of a sealing mastic where it enters the pipe. The bowl does not show signs of charring or carbon disposition.

RC296
Pipe, Effigy (Zoomorphic Bird)

Pipes - Figural Effigy

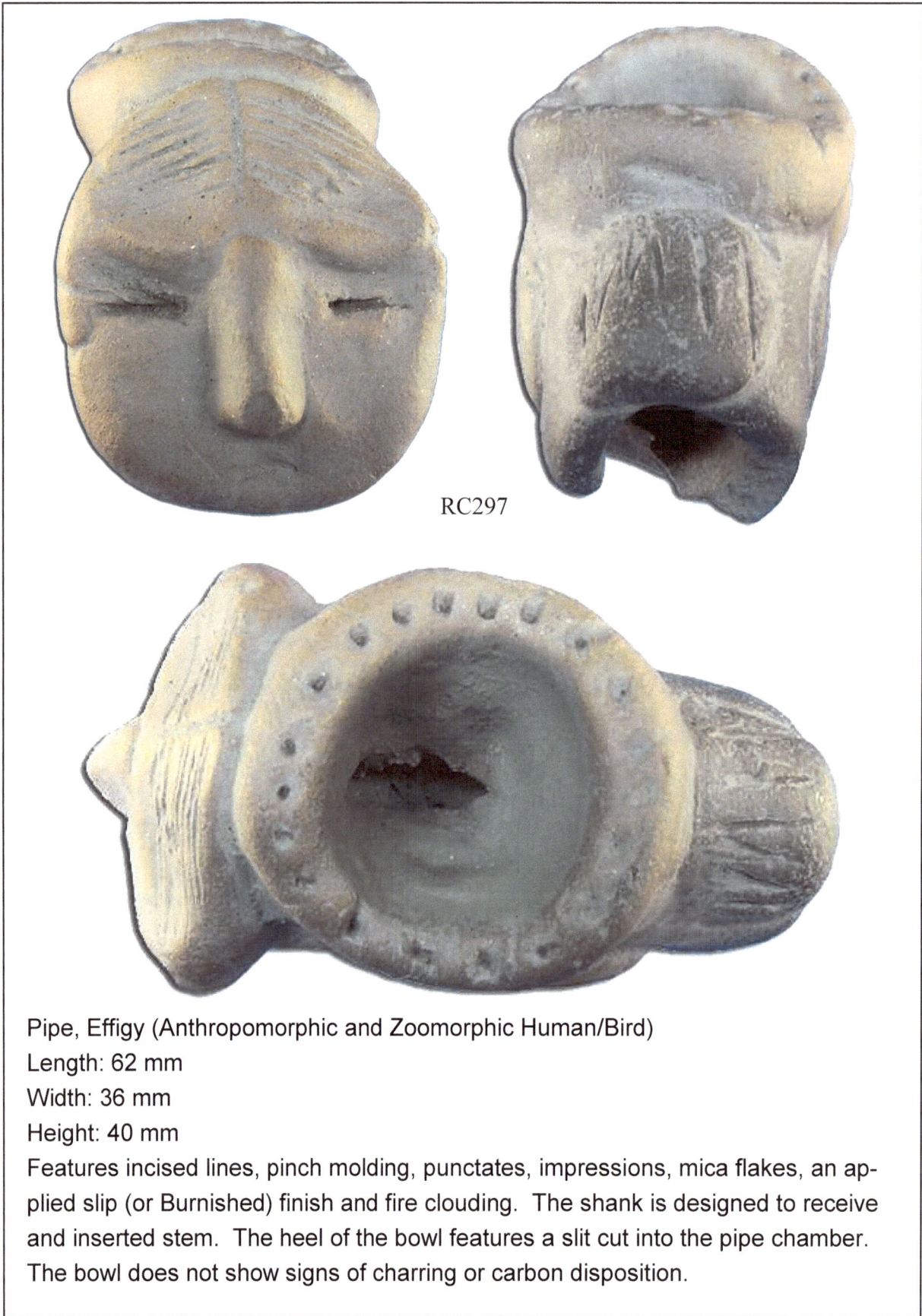

RC297

Pipe, Effigy (Anthropomorphic and Zoomorphic Human/Bird)

Length: 62 mm

Width: 36 mm

Height: 40 mm

Features incised lines, pinch molding, punctates, impressions, mica flakes, an applied slip (or Burnished) finish and fire clouding. The shank is designed to receive and inserted stem. The heel of the bowl features a slit cut into the pipe chamber. The bowl does not show signs of charring or carbon disposition.

Pipes - Figural Effigy

RC297
Pipe, Effigy (Anthropomorphic and Zoomorphic Human/Bird)

Pipes - Figural Effigy

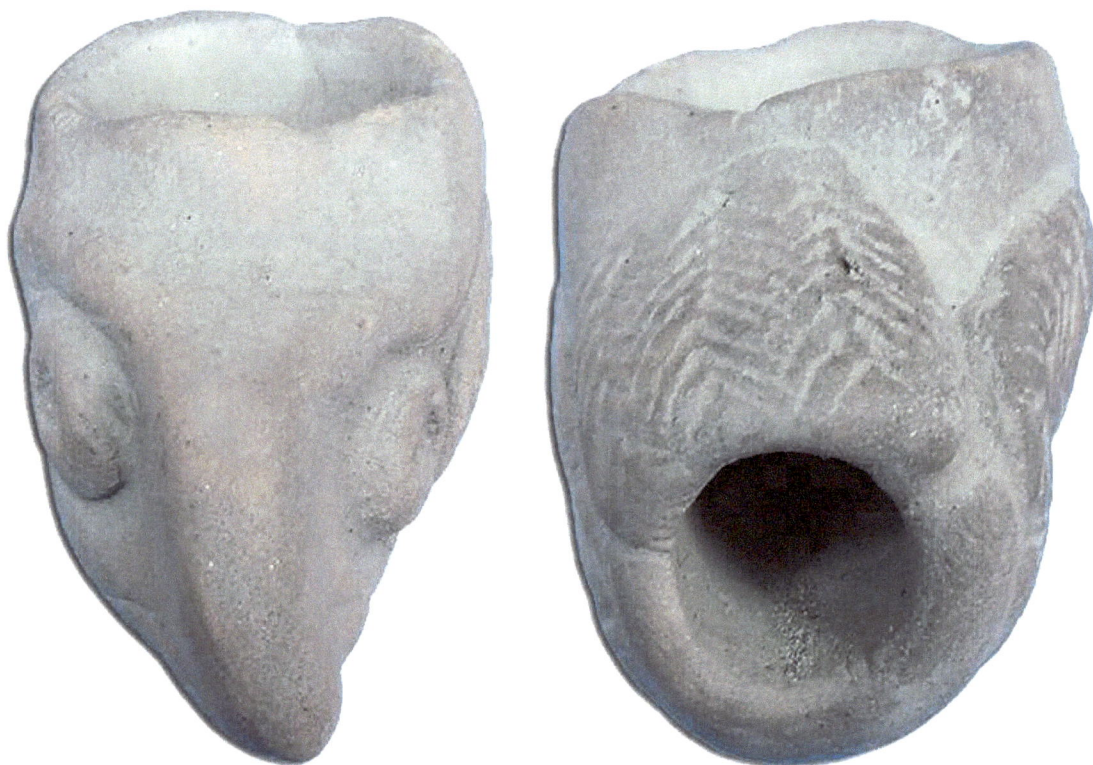

RC298

Pipe, Effigy (Zoomorphic Bird)
Length: 65 mm
Width: 30 mm
Height: 33 mm
Features incised lines, pinch molding, punctates, impressions, mica flakes, and an applied slip (or Burnished) finish. The shank is designed to receive and inserted stem. The heel of the bowl has been pierced to access the pipe chamber. The bowl does not show signs of charring or carbon disposition.

Pipes - Figural Effigy

RC298
Pipe, Effigy (Zoomorphic Bird)

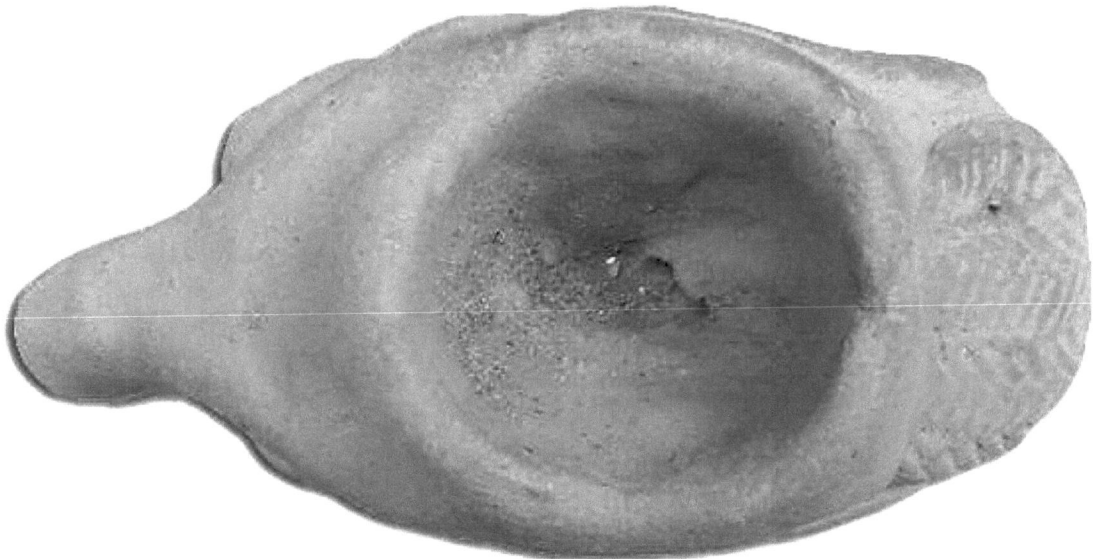

Pipes - Tube, Zoomorphic

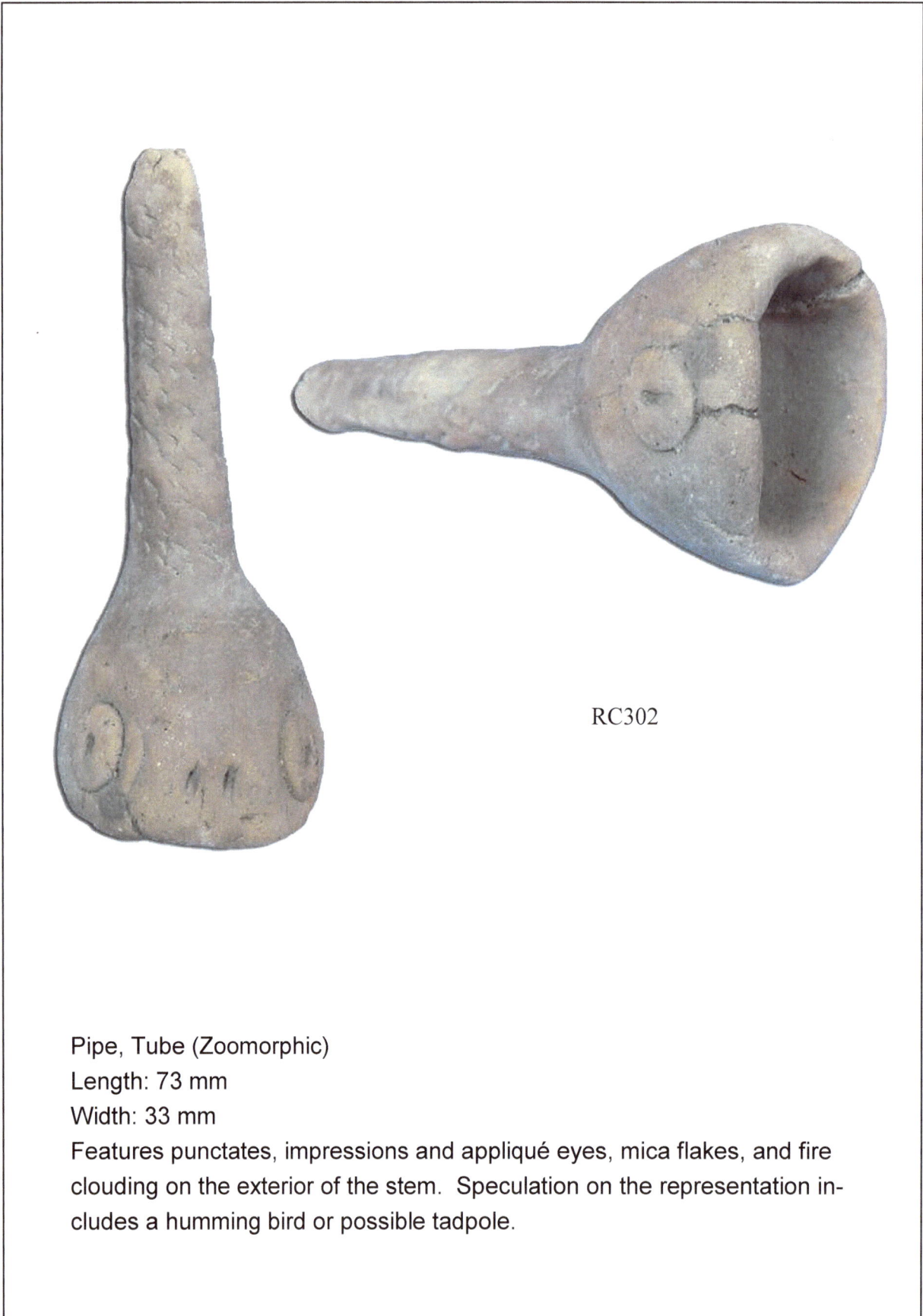

RC302

Pipe, Tube (Zoomorphic)
Length: 73 mm
Width: 33 mm
Features punctates, impressions and appliqué eyes, mica flakes, and fire
clouding on the exterior of the stem. Speculation on the representation in-
cludes a humming bird or possible tadpole.

Pipes - Tube, Zoomorphic

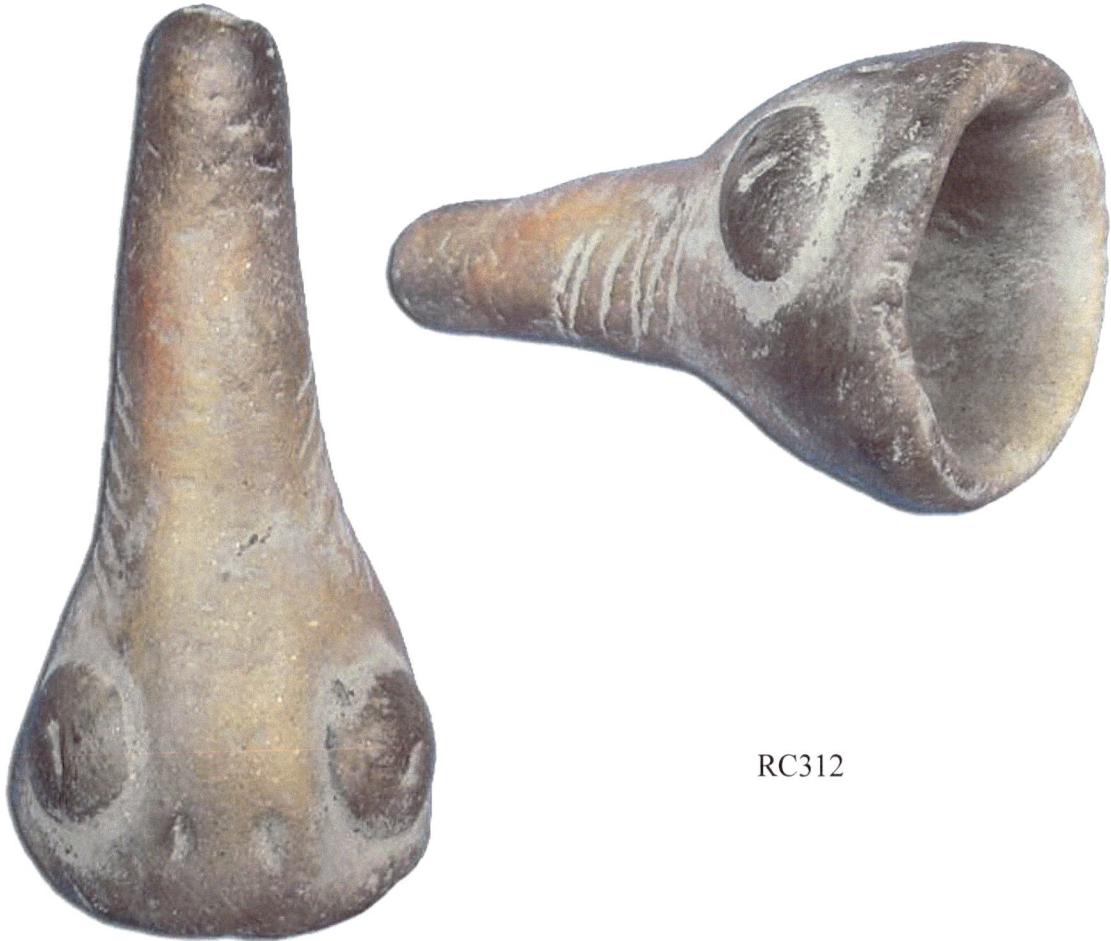

RC312

Pipe, Tube (Zoomorphic)
Length: 55 mm
Width: 28 mm
Features punctates, impressions and appliqué eyes, mica flakes, glossy burnished finish, and fire clouding on the exterior of the stem. Speculation on the representation includes a humming bird or possible tadpole.

Pipes - Tube, Zoomorphic

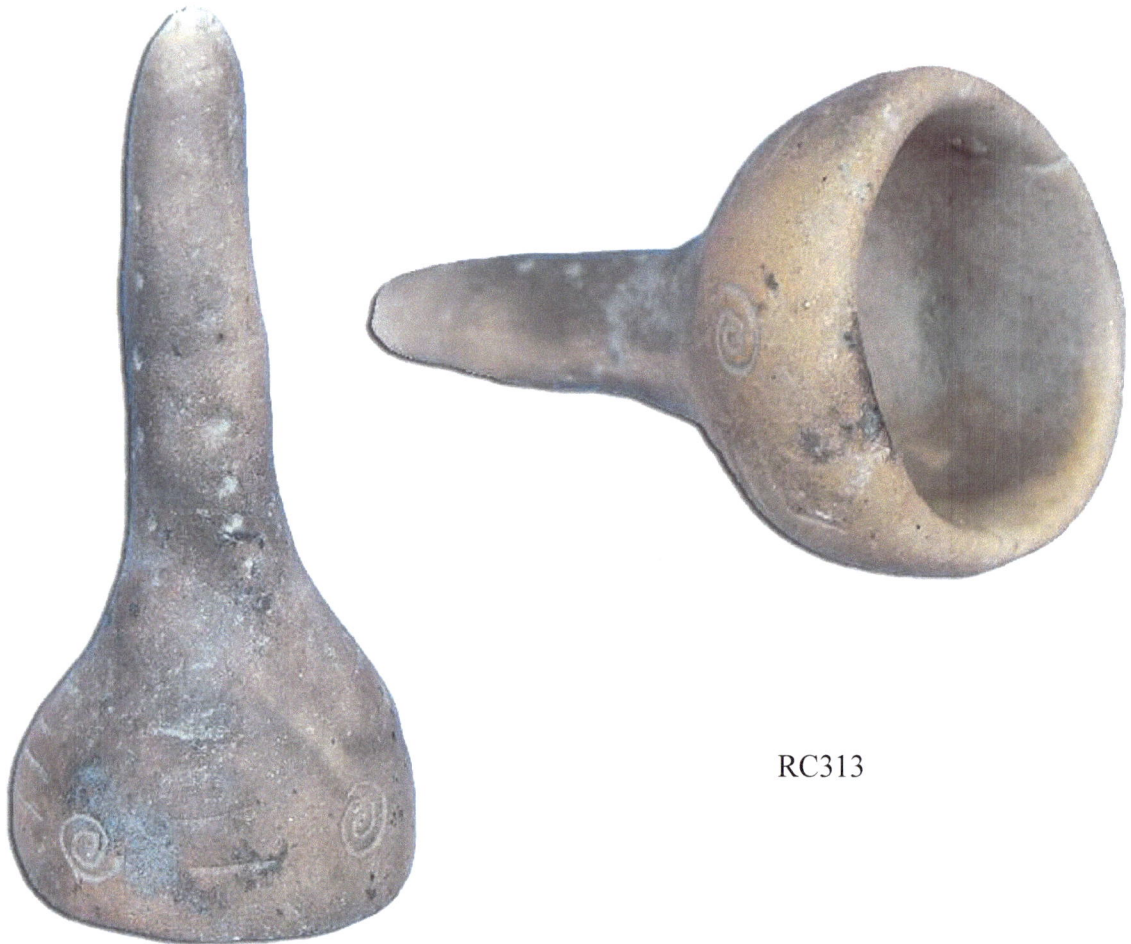

RC313

Pipe, Tube (Zoomorphic)
Length: 70 mm
Width: 35 mm
Features punctates, impressions and incised pin-wheel eyes, mica flakes, burnished finish, and fire clouding on the exterior of the stem. Speculation on the representation includes a humming bird or possible tadpole.

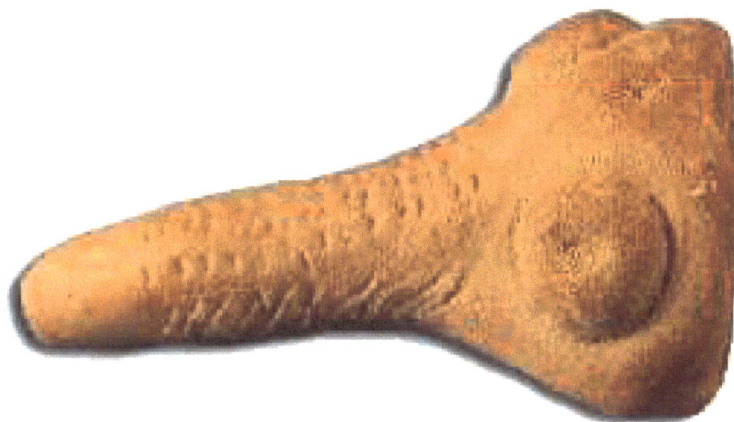

Pipes - Tube, Zoomorphic

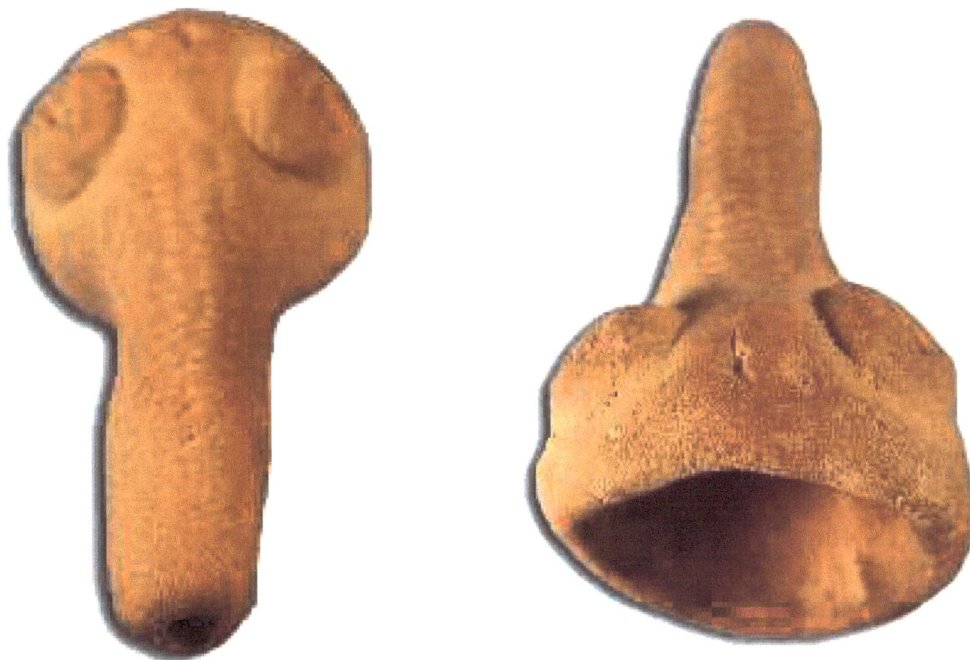

JSP1

Pipe, Tube (Zoomorphic)
Length: 78.5 mm
Width: 30 mm
Features punctates, impressions and appliqué eyes, mica flakes, the clay paste is coarse contain higher amounts of fine grained sand. Speculation on the representation includes a humming bird or possible tadpole. The bowl does show signs of charring or carbon disposition suggesting use.

Pipes - Tube, Expanding Stem

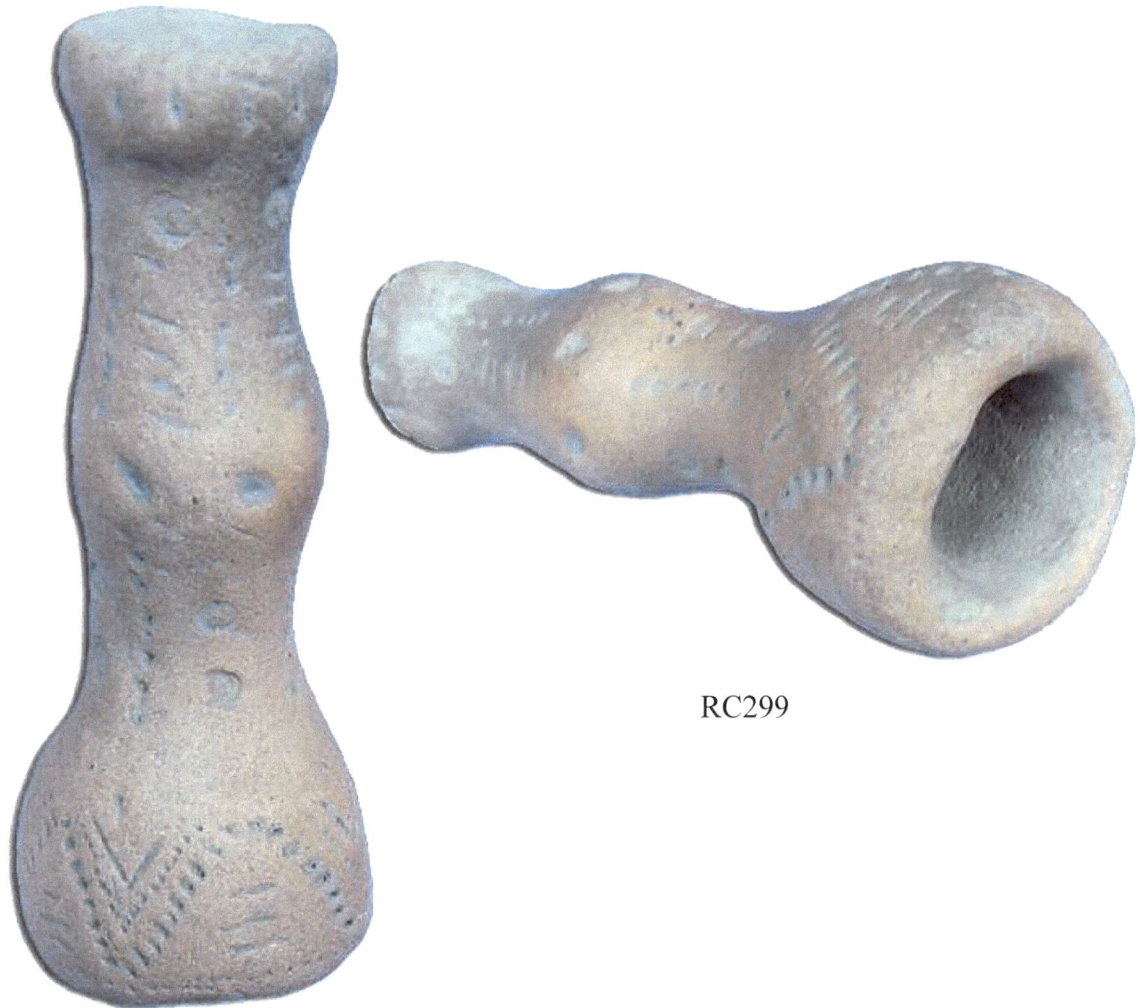

RC299

Pipe, Tube - Expanding Stem
Length: 66 mm
Width: 26 mm
Features geometric design with punctates and impressions, mica flakes,
burnished finish, and fire clouding on the exterior of the stem. The midpoint
of the stem is expanded.

RC300

Pipe, Tube - Expanding Stem
Length: 66 mm
Width: 26 mm
Features geometric design with incised lines, punctates and impressions, mica flakes, burnished finish, and fire clouding on the exterior of the stem. The midpoint of the stem is expanded.

Pipes - Tube, Expanding Stem

RC301

RC306

RC301 Pipe, Tube - Expanding Stem

Length: 75 mm

Width: 31 mm

Features geometric design with incised lines and punctates, mica flakes, burnished finish, and fire clouding on the exterior of the stem. The midpoint of the stem is expanded.

RC306 Pipe, Tube - Expanding Stem

Length: 65 mm

Width: 30 mm

Features geometric design with punctates and impressions, mica flakes, burnished finish, and fire clouding on the exterior of the stem. The midpoint of the stem is expanded.

Pipes - Tube, Expanding Stem

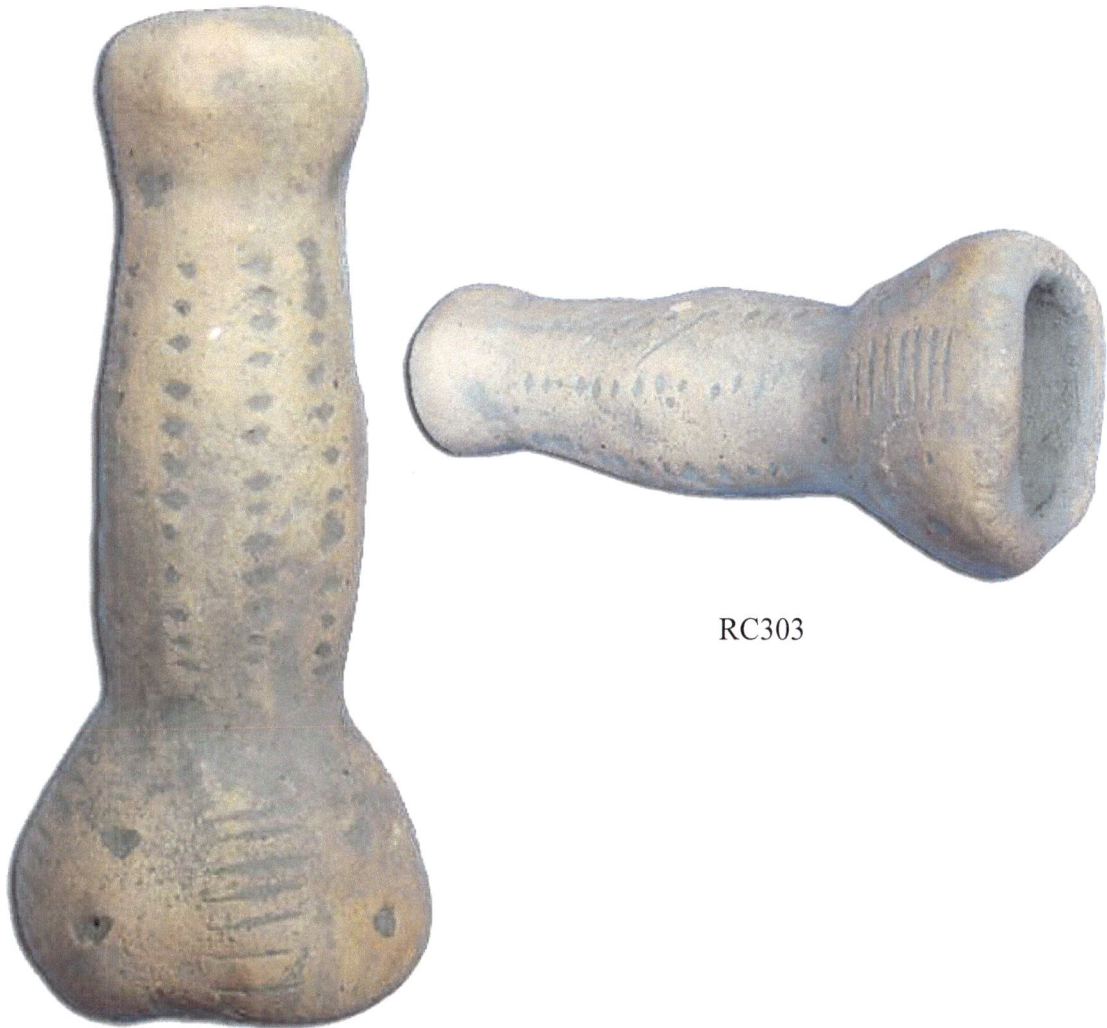

RC303

Pipe, Tube - Expanding Stem

Length: 60 mm

Width: 28 mm

Features geometric design with incised lines and impressions, mica flakes, burnished finish. The midpoint of the stem is expanded.

Pipes - Tube, Expanding Stem

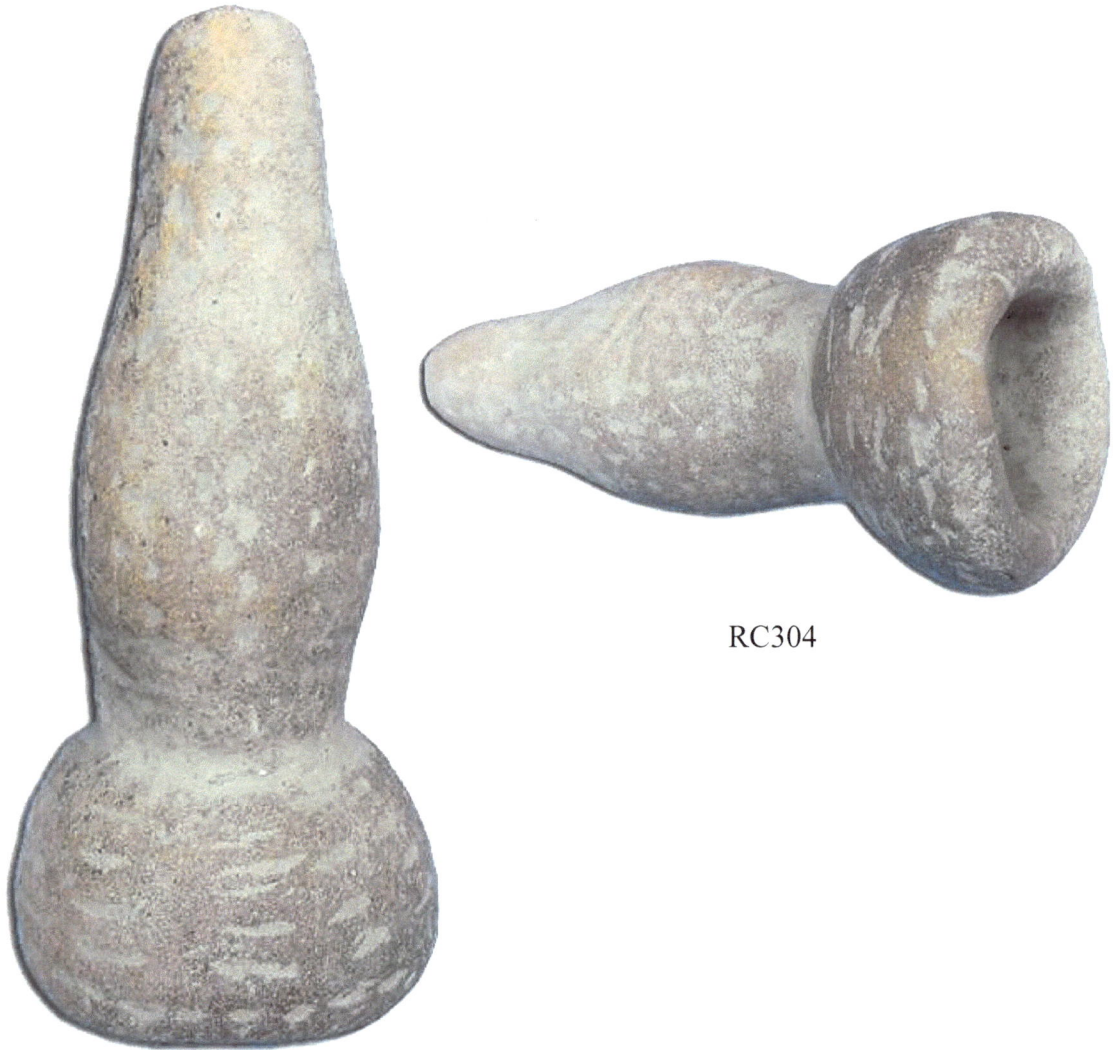

RC304

Pipe, Tube - Expanding Stem
Length: 68 mm
Width: 30 mm
Features geometric design with punctates and impressions, mica flakes, and fire clouding on the exterior of the stem. The midpoint of the stem is expanded.

Pipes - Tube, Expanding Stem

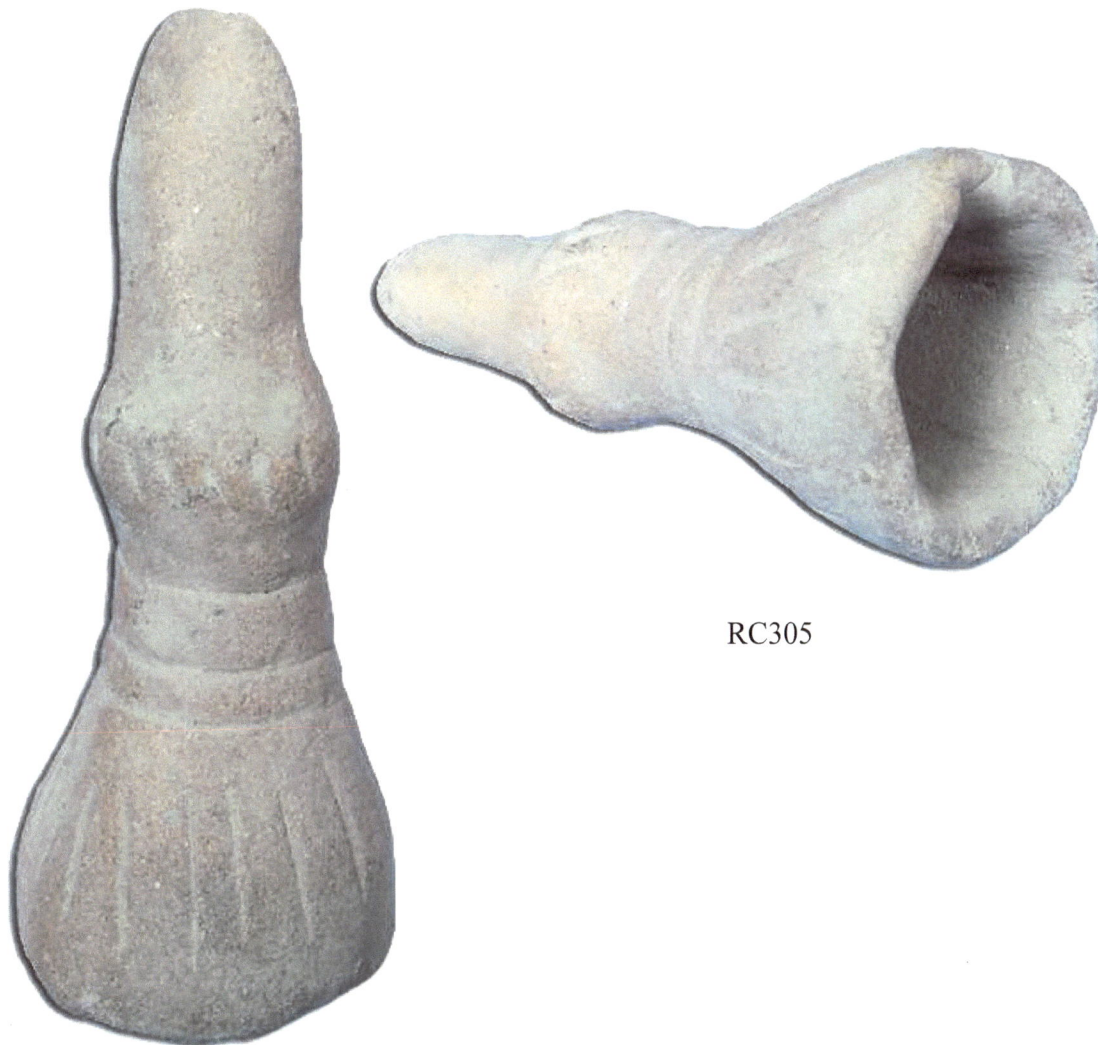

RC305

Pipe, Tube - Expanding Stem
Length: 60 mm
Width: 28 mm
Features geometric design with incised lines and impressions and mica flakes. The midpoint of the stem is expanded.

Pipes - Tube, Expanding Stem

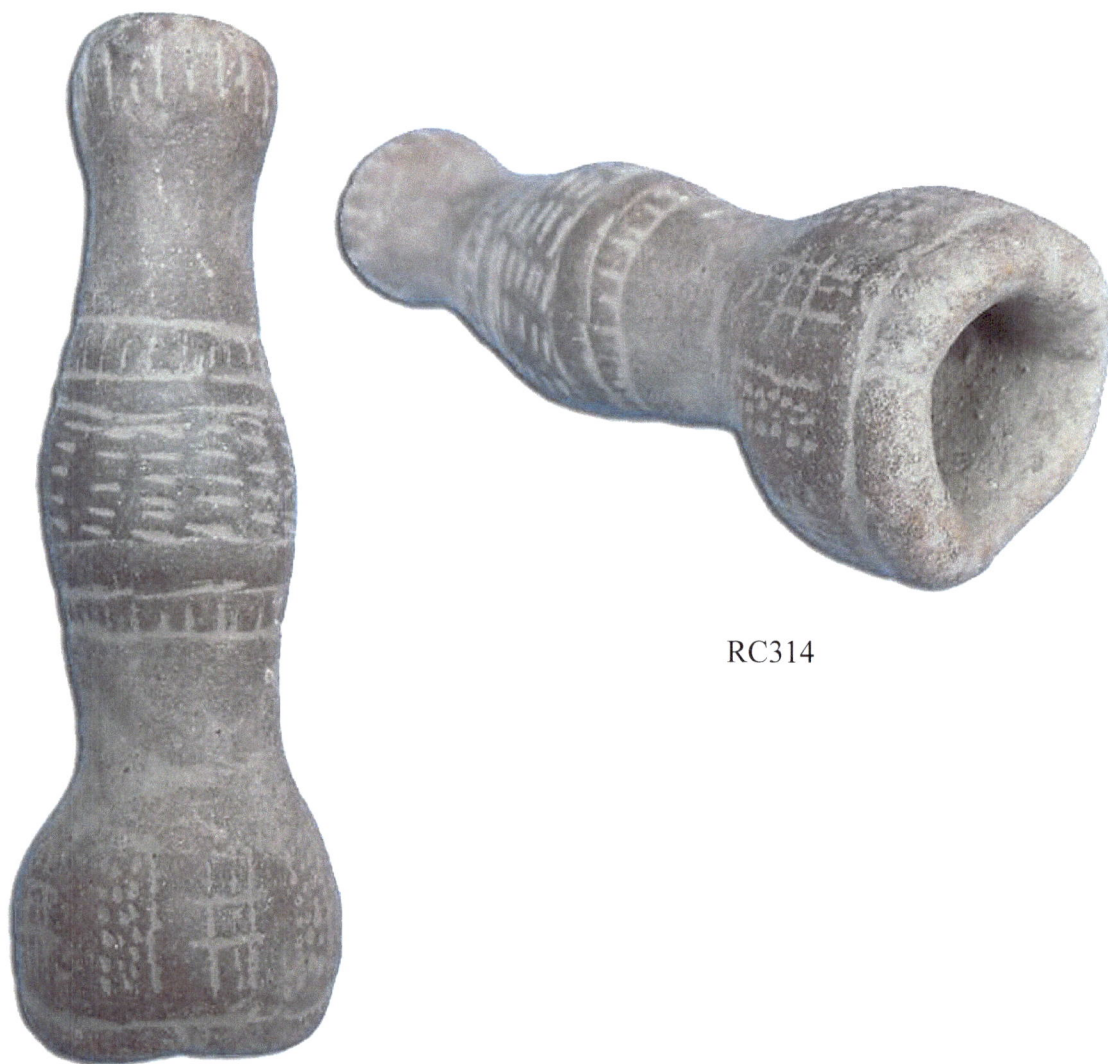

RC314

Pipe, Tube - Expanding Stem
Length: 76 mm
Width: 26 mm
Features geometric design with incised lines, punctates and impressions, mica flakes, burnished finish, and fire clouding on the exterior of the stem. The midpoint of the stem is expanded.

Pipes - Tube, Long Stem

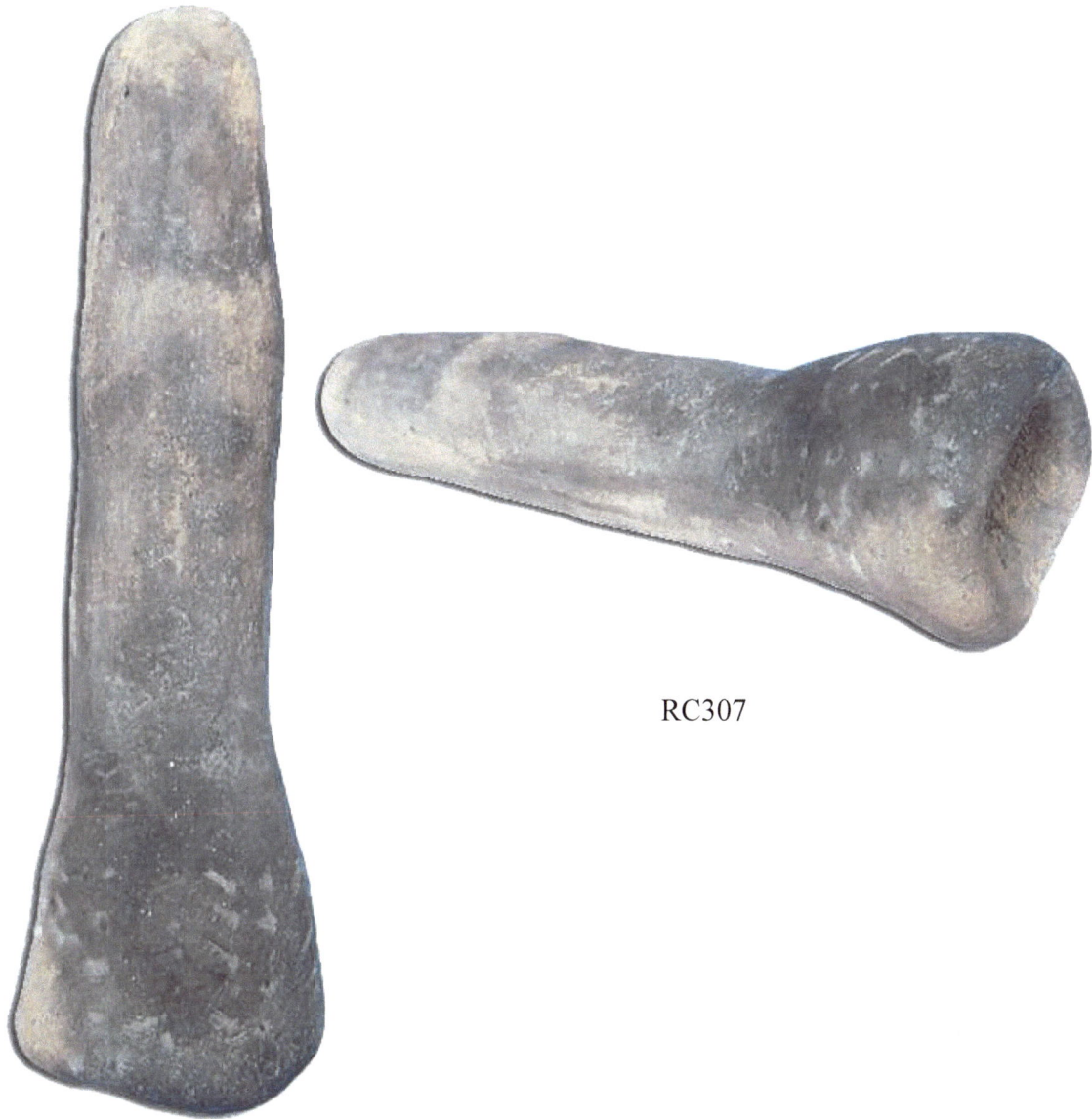

RC307

Pipe, Tube - Long Stem
Length: 75 mm
Width: 22 mm
Features geometric chevron designs with punctates and impressions, mica flakes, burnished finish, and fire clouding on the exterior of the stem, featured secondary modification as evidenced by stem scraping around the entire circumference of the stem.

Pipes - Tube, Long Stem

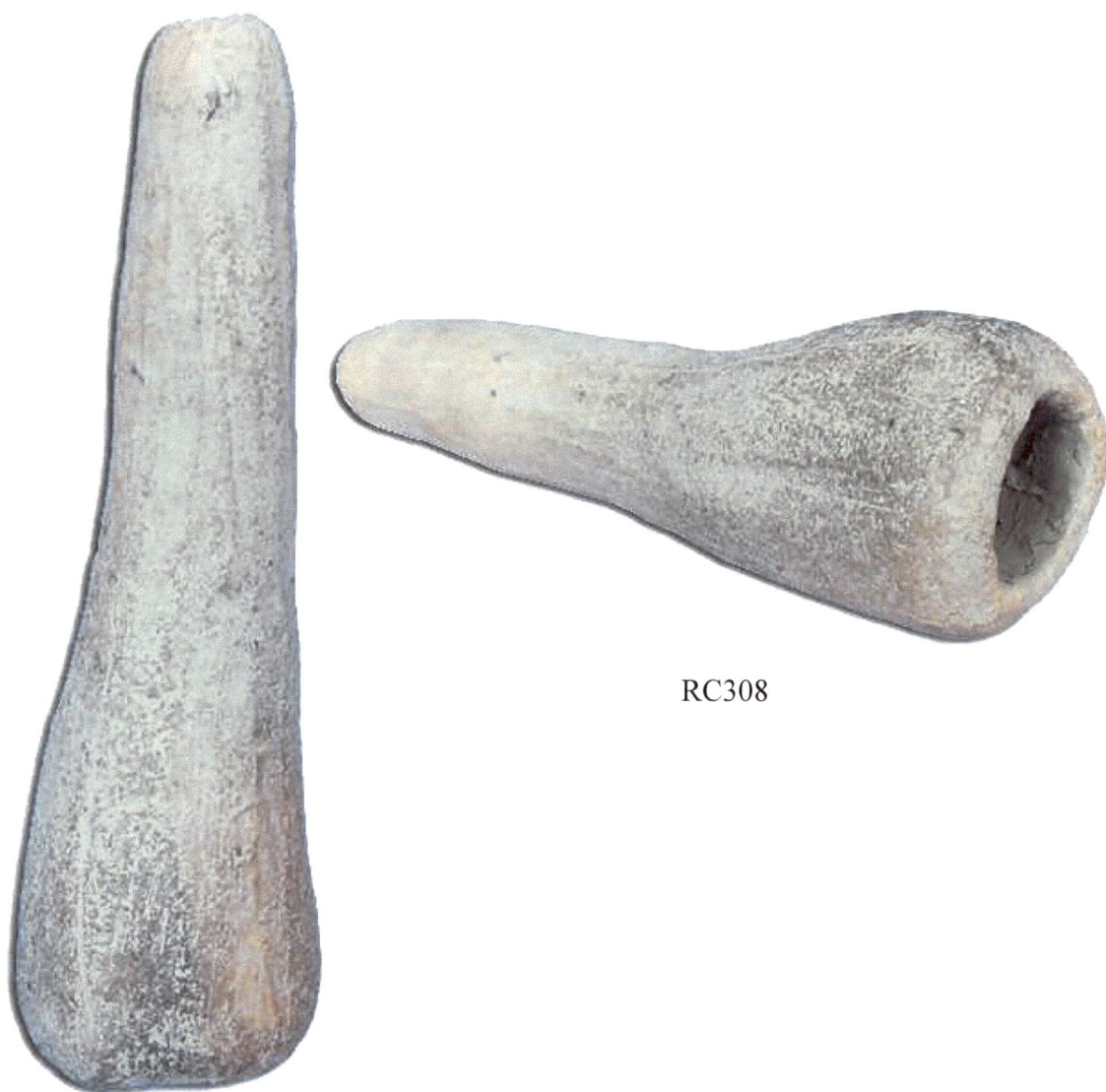

RC308

Pipe, Tube - Long Stem
Length: 67 mm
Width: 20 mm
Undecorated, mica flakes, burnished finish, and fire clouding on the exterior of the stem, featured secondary modification as evidenced by stem scraping around the entire circumference of the stem.

Pipes - Tube, Long Stem

AAHP2

Pipe, Tube - Long Stem
Length: 61 mm
Width: 16 mm max.
Undecorated, mica flakes, burnished finish, and fire clouding on the exterior of the stem, featured secondary modification as evidenced by stem scraping around the entire circumference of the stem.

RC309

Pipe, Tube - Short Stem
Length: 39 mm
Width: 25 mm
Features geometric design with incised lines, punctates and impressions, mica flakes, and fire clouding on the exterior.

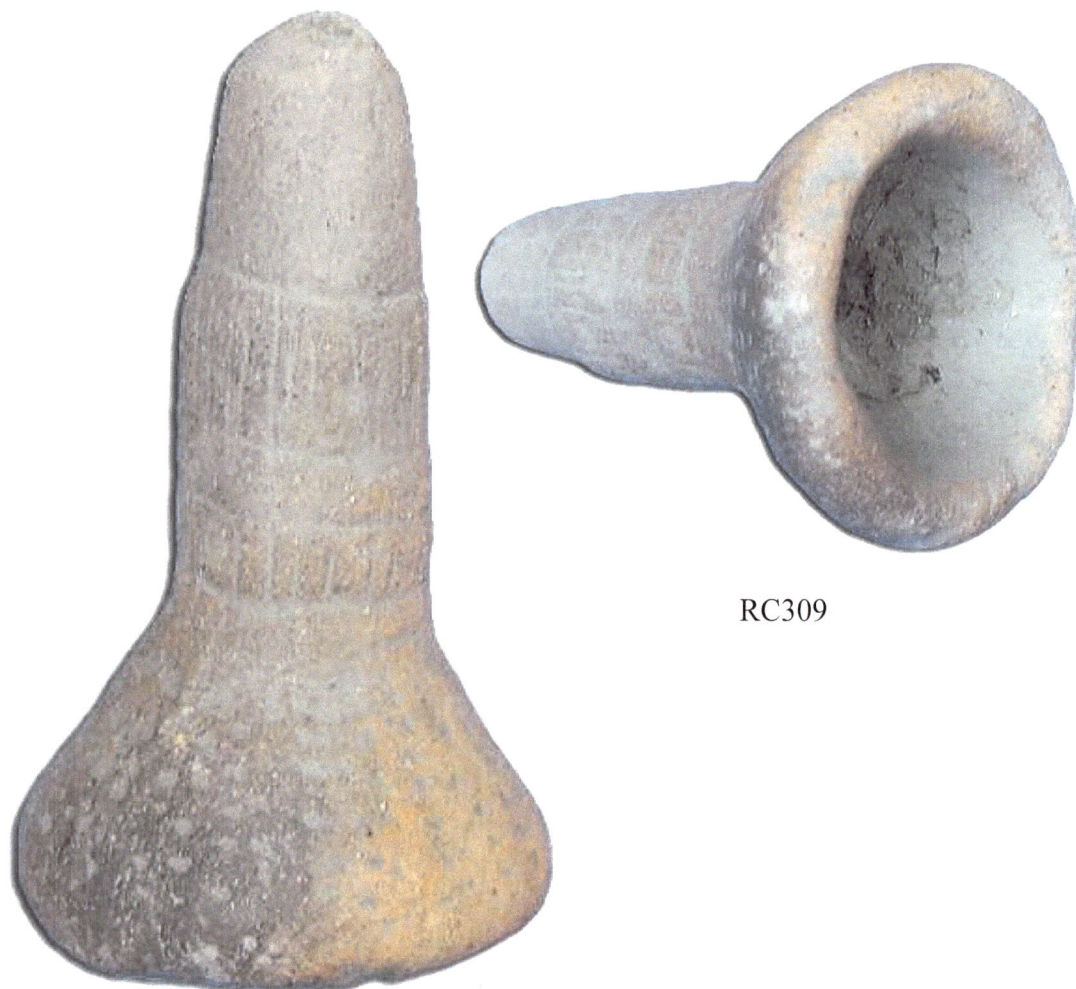

Pipes - Tube, Short Stem

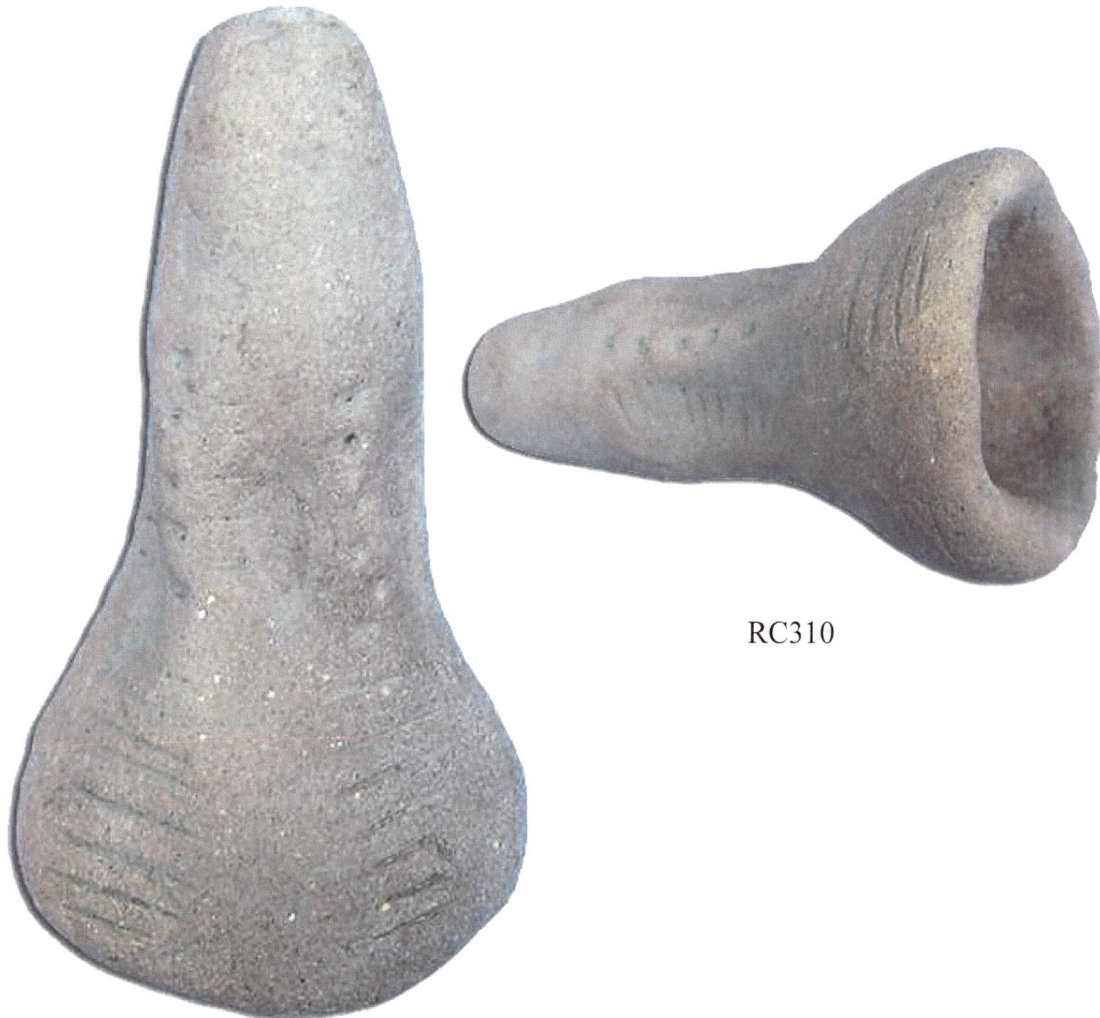

RC310

Pipe, Tube - Short Stem
Length: 39 mm
Width: 33 mm
Features geometric design with incised lines, punctates and impressions, mica flakes, and pinch molded stem feature.

Pipes - Tube, Short Stem

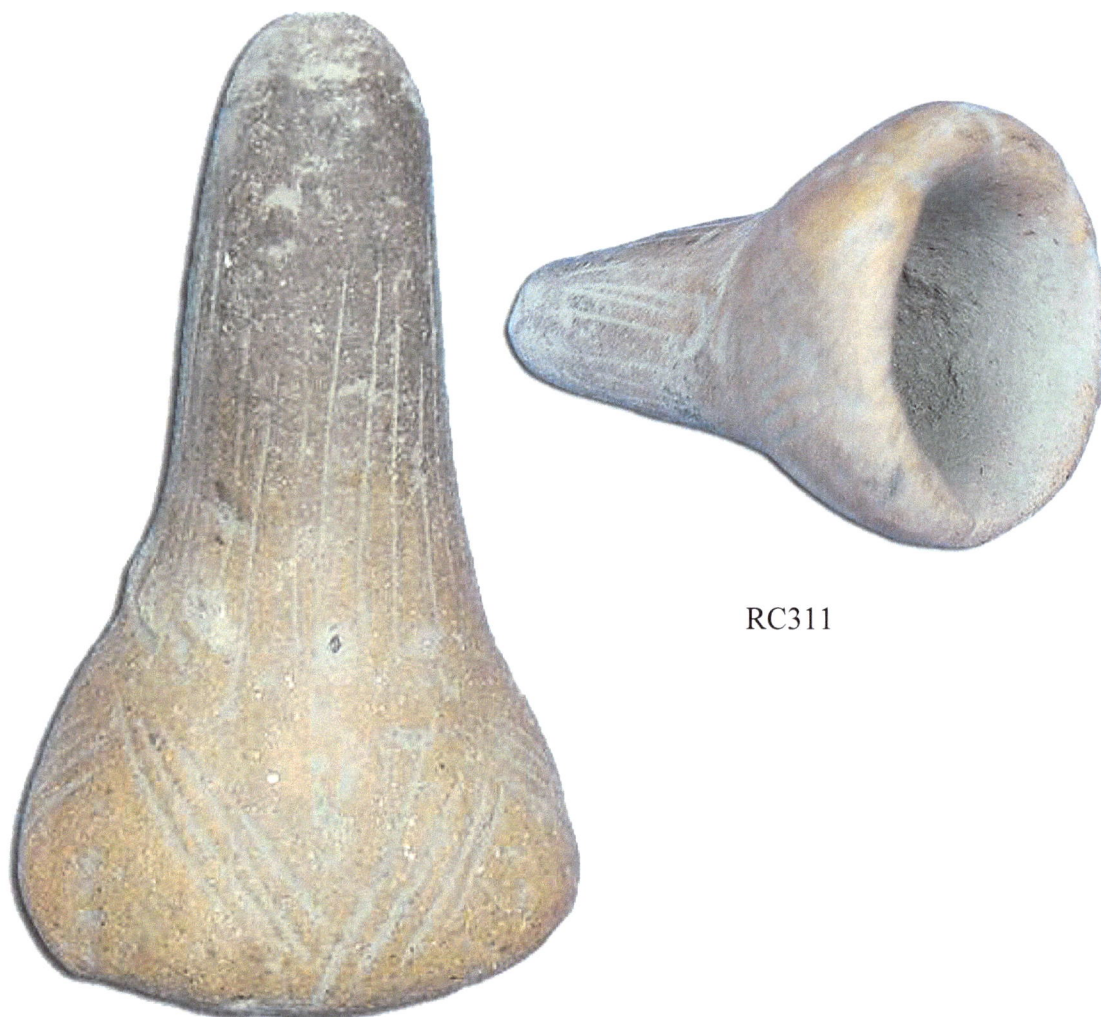

RC311

Pipe, Tube - Short Stem
Length: 43 mm
Width: 27 mm
Features geometric design with incised lines, punctates and impressions, mica flakes, glossy exterior, and fire clouding on the exterior.

Pipes - Tube, Short Stem

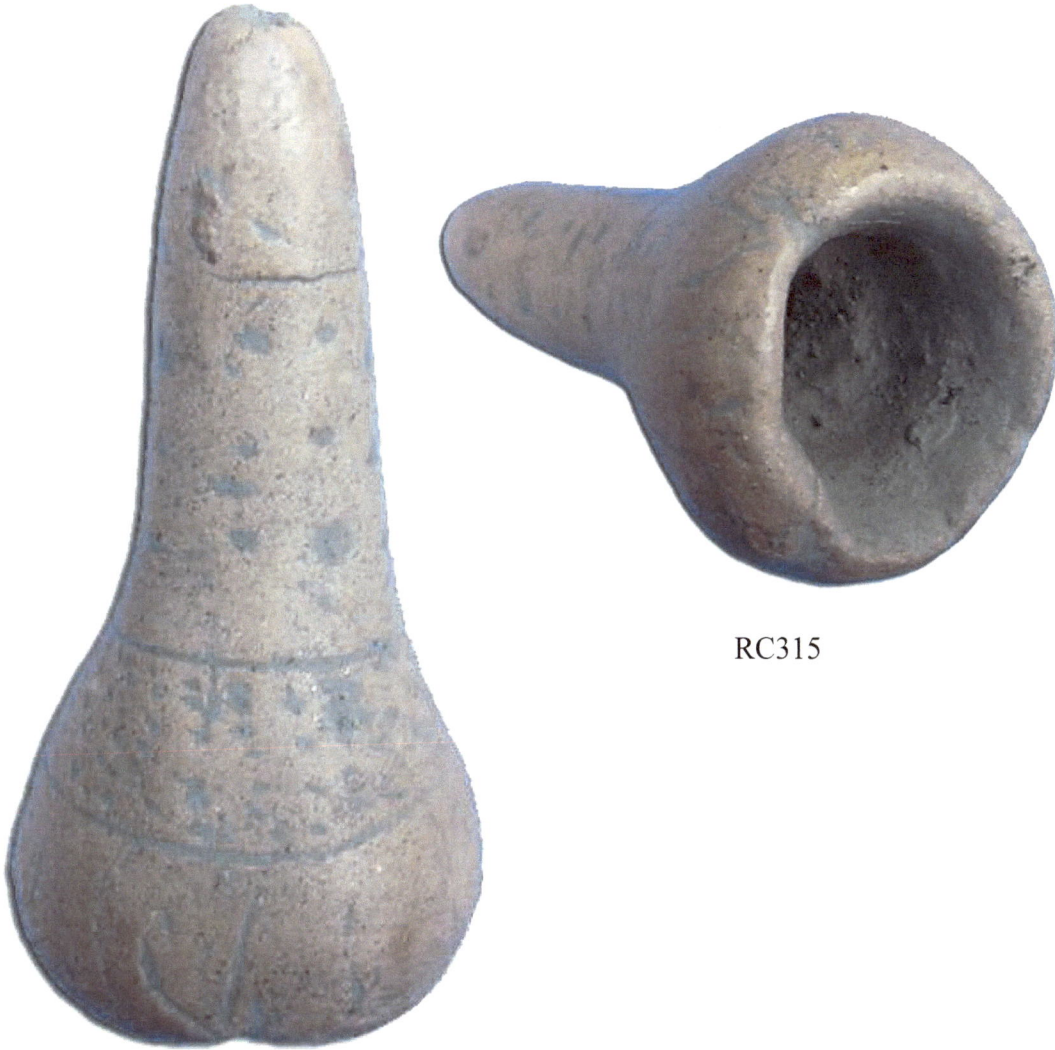

RC315

Pipe, Tube - Short Stem

Length: 43 mm

Width: 22 mm

Features geometric design with incised lines, punctates and impressions, mica flakes, glossy exterior.

Pipes - Tube, Short Stem

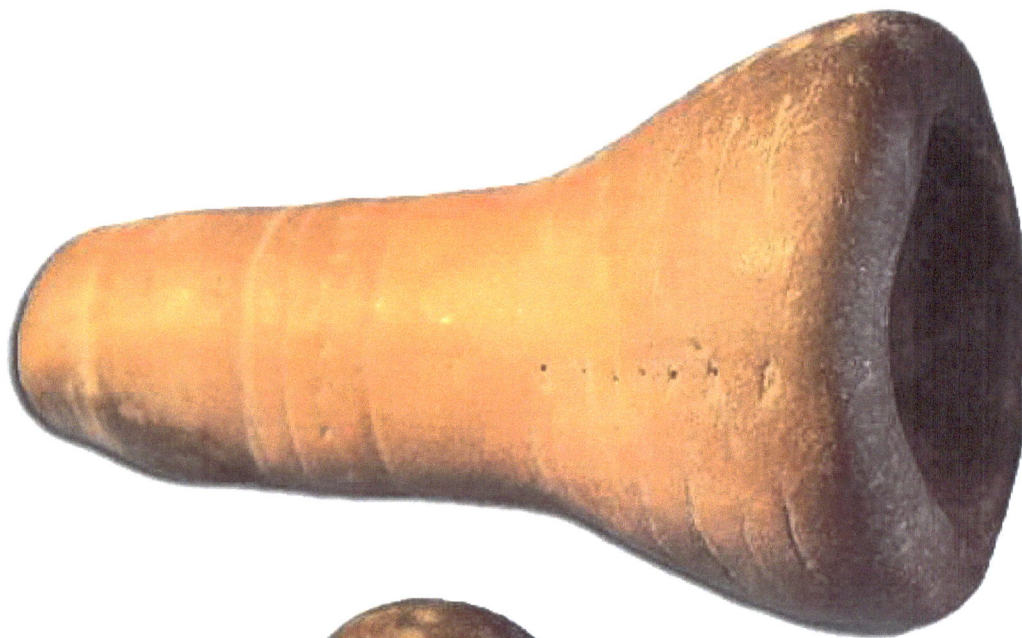

AAHP1

Pipe, Tube - Short Stem
Length: 46 mm
Width: 25.5 mm (inner bowl diameter 15 mm)
Features geometric design with incised lines, punctates and impressions, mica flakes, glossy exterior. Recovered at the Herzog site (45CL11)

Pipes - Tube, Short Stem

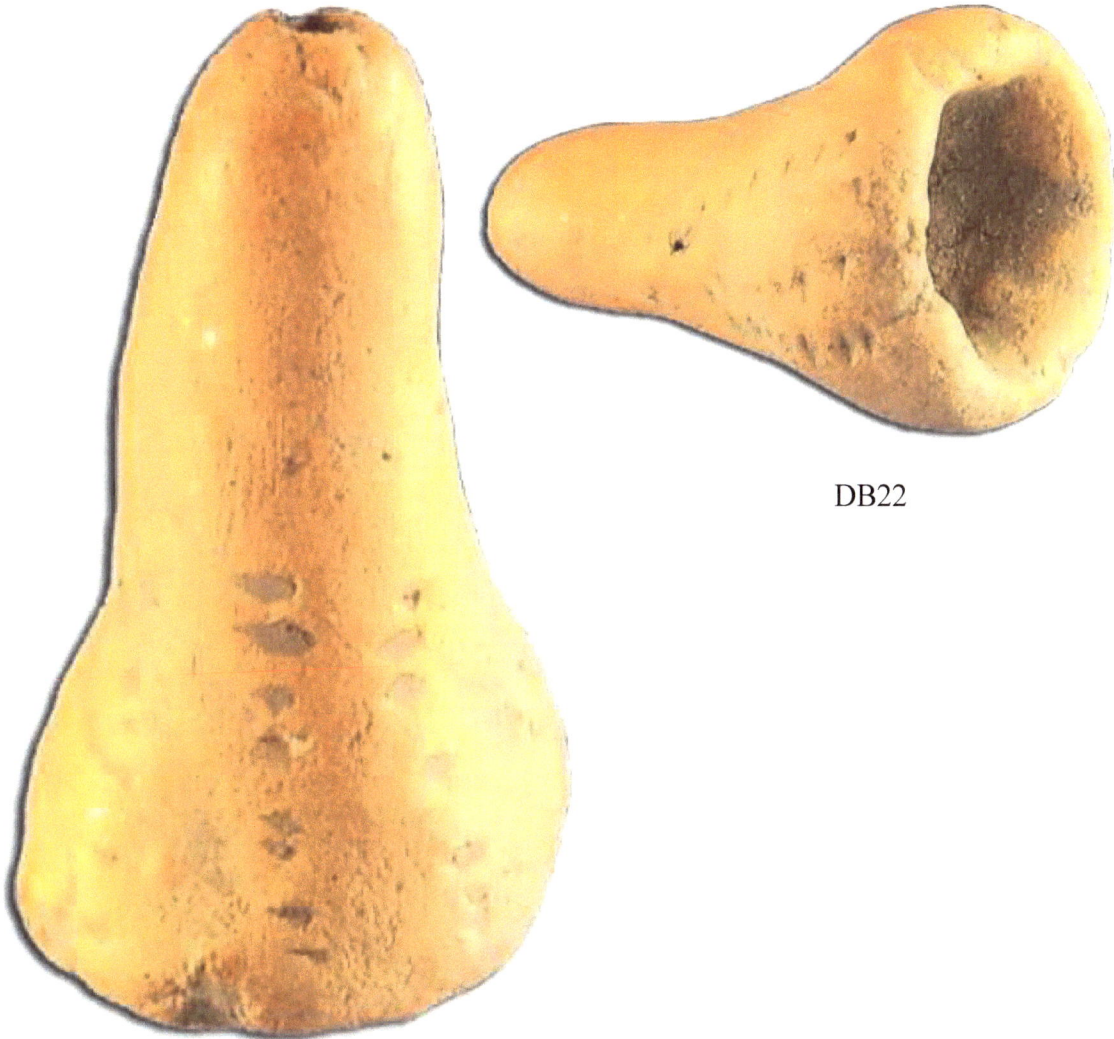

DB22

Pipe, Tube - Short Stem
Length: 40 mm
Width: 24 mm
Features geometric design with punctates and impressions, mica flakes, glossy exterior.

Pipes - Elbow

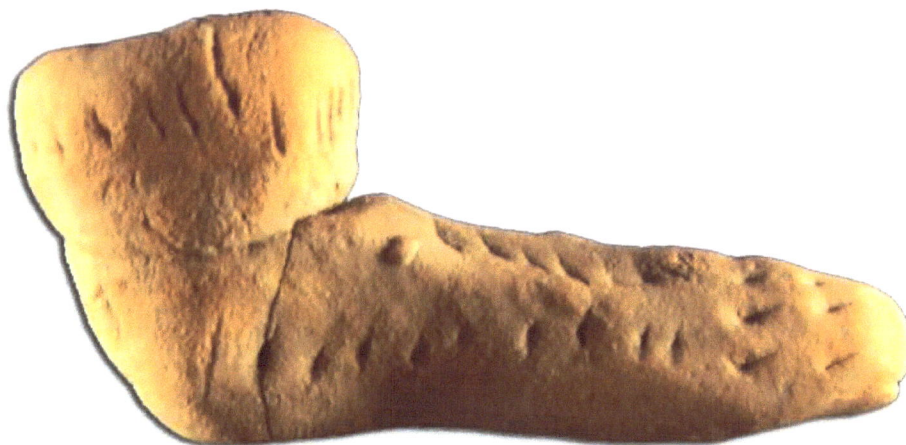

AAHP3

Pipe, Elbow

Length: 76.5 mm

Stem Width: 21 mm

Bowl: 28 mm OD, 21 mm ID

Features geometric design with punctates and impressions, mica flakes, two-piece construction with an applied bowl. Recovered at the Herzog site (45CL11)

Clarifications of Terms

Burnished Finish appears on many of the ceramics and often gives the ware a polished appearance. Some of these burnishing is very fine and prevents water absorption. There has been some speculation that perhaps some form of applied treatment was added to the ware surface. This has yet to be confirmed and a point of future research.

Clay Paste used to construct these wares appears to be from local sources located on Lake River. Analysis indicates tempers or fillers were not added to the clay paste prior to manufacture. The paste characteristics are uniform, highly plastic and homogeneous, often containing naturally occurring opening materials such as fine-grained sands and mica flecks.

Fire Clouding is a term used to describe depositioned carbon on the ceramics surface. This typically occurs during the firing process and may suggest the ceramic was in contact with the smoky part of the flame or incompletely burnt fuel source.

Grey Slip Finish appears on many of the ceramics and often mutes the decorative motifs. The appearance suggests a slurry type clay mixture that was rubbed over the surface of the ware.

Lake River Ceramics is a term put forth by Dr. Alison Stenger of the Institute for Archaeological Studies, Portland Oregon (Stenger, 2002). This term has gained acceptance in the archaeological community.

Shoto Clay was the name first applied to the ceramic wares found at Lake River by Robert Slocum and Kenneth Matsen (1968). This is the term most commonly used by those who maintain privately held collections. Ken confirmed the term, "Shoto Clay," was not intended to say the Shoto peoples made these wares (comm., 2008). Rather, it was intended as a location reference that directly relates to Lewis and Clark's historically recorded observation of the people who occupied the upper stretches of Lake River in 1806.

Smudging is a coloring technique used to blacken the ceramic ware. This is typically done by exposing the finished ware to the smoky part of the flame, not to be confused with fire clouding.

References

Heath, David
2004 to Current Personal Research Notes, unpublished.

2009   Prehistoric Ceramic Wares From The Lower Columbia River, unpublished.

Hoffarber, Ray
1969   Felida Site (CL6), Screenings, Oregon Archaeological Society, Vol. 18(9) and Vol. 18(10)

Matsen, Kenneth
1966   Clay Artifacts, Screenings, Oregon Archaeological Society, Vol. 15(7)

2008 to current - Personal Communications.

Osborne, Douglas
1957   Pottery in the Northwest, American Antiquity, Vol. 23(1).

Pettigrew, Richard M.
1981   A Prehistoric Culture Sequence in the Portland Basin of the Lower Columbia Valley, University of Oregon Anthropological Papers, No. 22

Slocum, Robert
1968   Lower Columbia River Figurines - A possible Cultural Indicator For The Northwest, PSU, Prehistory of the Northwest, Anthro. 407, Dr. Thomas M. Newman

Slocum, Robert; Matsen, Kenneth
1968   Shoto Clay, A Description of Clay Artifacts From The Herzog Site (45-CL-4) In the Lower Columbia Region, Oregon Archaeological Society, No. 4

1972   Duck Lake - Archaeological Site Report 45-CL6A), Oregon Archaeological Society, No. 6

Stenger, Alison T.
1990   Japanese Influenced Ceramics in Pre-contact Washington ... New World Figurine Project 1: 111-122

2002   Prehistoric Ceramics From Southwest Washington, Screenings, Oregon Archaeological Society, Vol. 51 (7)

2008 to current - Personal Communications.

2009   A Vanished People - The Lake River Ceramic Makers, Institute for Archaeological Studies, Portland Oregon

Strong, Emory
1959   Stone Age on the Columbia River, Binfords and Mort Publishers

Wilbert, Claire T.
2010   Confronting Unprovenienced Collections: A Case Study Of Lake River Ceramics From The Columbia River Region Of The Northwest Coast, Scripps College, Undergraduate Program, Prof. Chen

NOTES

www.ingramcontent.com/pod-product-compliance
Lightning Source LLC
Chambersburg PA
CBHW060810270326
41928CB00002B/48